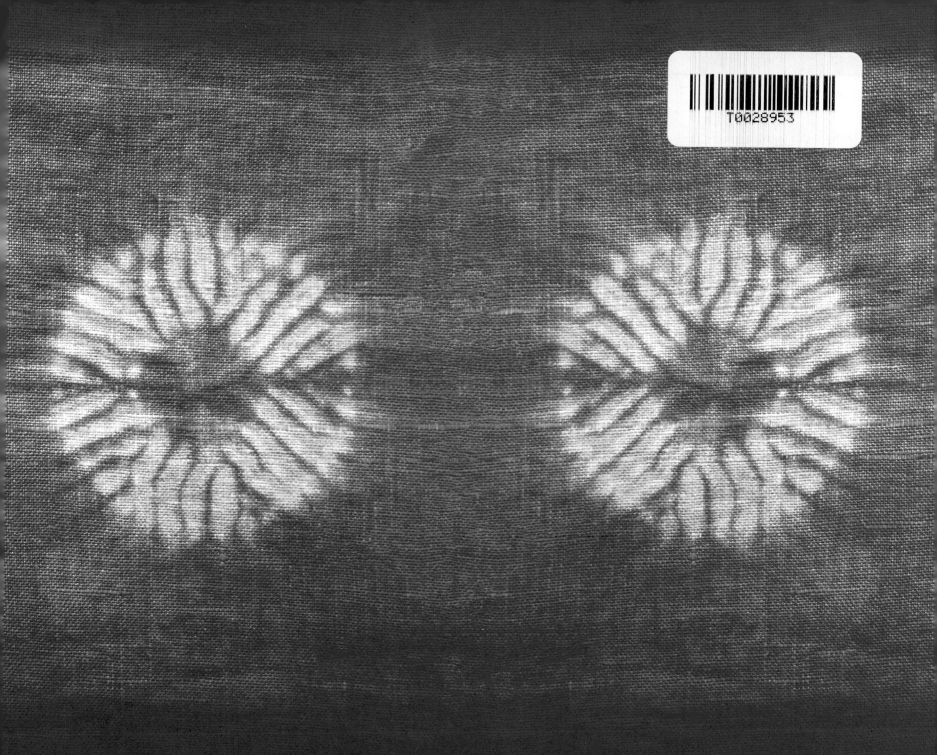

My Indigo World

A True Story of the Color Blue

Rosa Chang

mineditionUS

I was a daydreamer when I was
a girl growing up in Korea.
I would look out the window
and always see blue.
I fell in love with the color blue.

In autumn, there was the strong shade of blue sky we called jjok. There was the blue stripe sitting among the other colors on my baby hanbok, a traditional Korean garment.

My first trip to Jeju Island with my grandma and mom
was full of excitement. That's when I first saw for myself
how the blue of the sky meets the blue of the sea.

And I remember seeing the darkest blue of all in the night sky during a camping trip in the woods.

I was a grown-up living in the United States when a friend gave me a handful of *seeds* from a *special* plant growing in his backyard. The next morning, I planted the seeds in my own garden, not realizing these indigo seeds would change my life.

Kimono from Japan

Fabric from West Africa

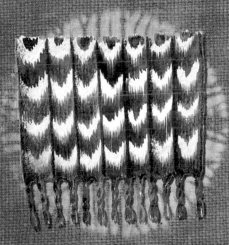

Handwoven rug
from Guatemala

Denim jeans

I soon learned that people around the world had been growing indigo plants for centuries. It's from the leaves of these plants that the most beautiful blue dyes have long been made.

The blue used for traditional Japanese kimonos. The blue for which West Africa's most highly prized fabrics are known. The deep and soulful blue found in Guatemalan handwoven rugs. Even blue jeans were once dyed blue using indigo!

Now I grow indigo plants with my friends
on a little farm in the middle of Baltimore.

You might wonder, how can such a small plant with leaves so green be the source of this amazing, deep shade of blue for the people of the world? Come join us and we'll show you!

Early in the spring, we plant indigo seeds indoors. We fill the seedling trays—sometimes plastic egg cartons or yogurt containers—with potting soil. Then we put in the seeds and place the trays in a sunny place in our homes.

Once the indigo plants sprout, we take them outdoors and replant them in the garden. Earthworms help make the soil nice and loose.

Other animals, for instance, chickens from a neighbor's garden, help enrich the soil too—with their poop!

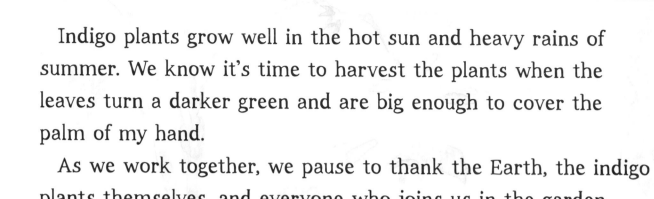

Indigo plants grow well in the hot sun and heavy rains of summer. We know it's time to harvest the plants when the leaves turn a darker green and are big enough to cover the palm of my hand.

As we work together, we pause to thank the Earth, the indigo plants themselves, and everyone who joins us in the garden.

Next, we cut down the indigo stalks and gather the leaves. The ground may look bare, but in a month's time the plants will have grown back for us to harvest again.

But how do we get a blue dye from these green plants? The answer is, with the help of a secret ingredient that lives inside the indigo leaves. It's called indican. When it mixes with the oxygen in water, the process of creating indigo dye begins.

WATER

WEIGHTS

INDIGO LEAVES

AROUND TWO DAYS LATER, WE NOTICE THE WATER CHANGING TO GREENISH YELLOW

WATER

INDIGO LEAVES

ROCKS / PEBBLES

We put our harvested leaves in jars or pots, add water, place heavy stones on top of the leaves, and wait. Can you see the color of the water starting to change?

A few days later, we return to remove the stones and leaves, and look! The water has turned a beautiful turquoise color! All this color has come from the leaves. But it is still not the blue we want.

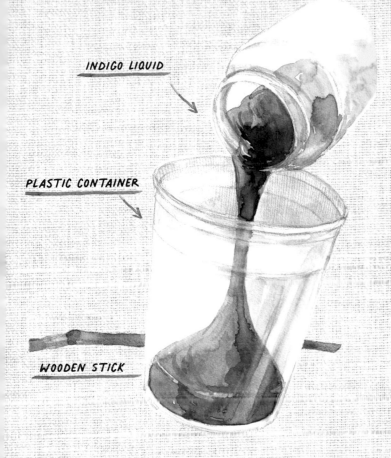

INDIGO LIQUID

PLASTIC CONTAINER

WOODEN STICK

To deepen the blue color, we now pour the liquid into a big container and stir it with a wooden stick. We want the liquid to mix with the oxygen in the air. We want the liquid to breathe!

PICKLING LIME /
CALCIUM HYDROXIDE

MIX IT WELL TO
LET THE AIR IN.

Next, we add one more special ingredient: calcium hydroxide, or pickling lime, which is another chemical found in nature. Here in Baltimore, we buy pickling lime at the store, but my ancestors in Korea made it themselves by grinding burned oyster shells or other seashells.

As we keep stirring the mixture, we catch glimpses of a rainbow of colors in the turquoise water: sky blue, dandelion yellow, purple, and green!

At last, we see it at the bottom of the pot—the color I call the Real Blue: a dense and rich blue paste, the bluest blue of all.

In Korea, we call this treasured blue shade niram. This is a magical time! Everyone gathers in the garden with whatever they want to dye with indigo.

Now our indigo garden is aglow with the beautiful blue shade of niram.

While we admire each other's work, we learn about what indigo means to each of us.

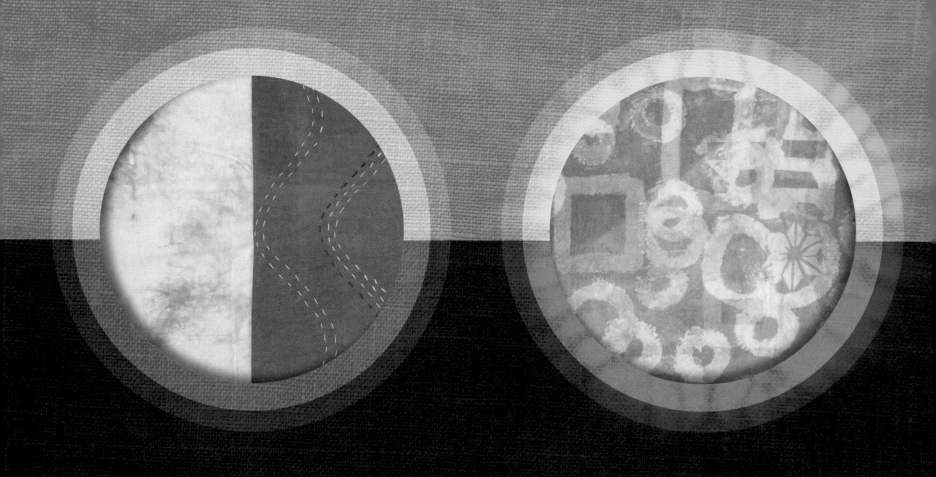

"Indigo means community. It means sharing stories with friends."

"To me, indigo is a treasure we pass down to our children."

"Indigo is the color of love.
It's the color of healing, and it's
deeper than any other blue."

"I think indigo is the color in which
lives the spirit and soul of my people."

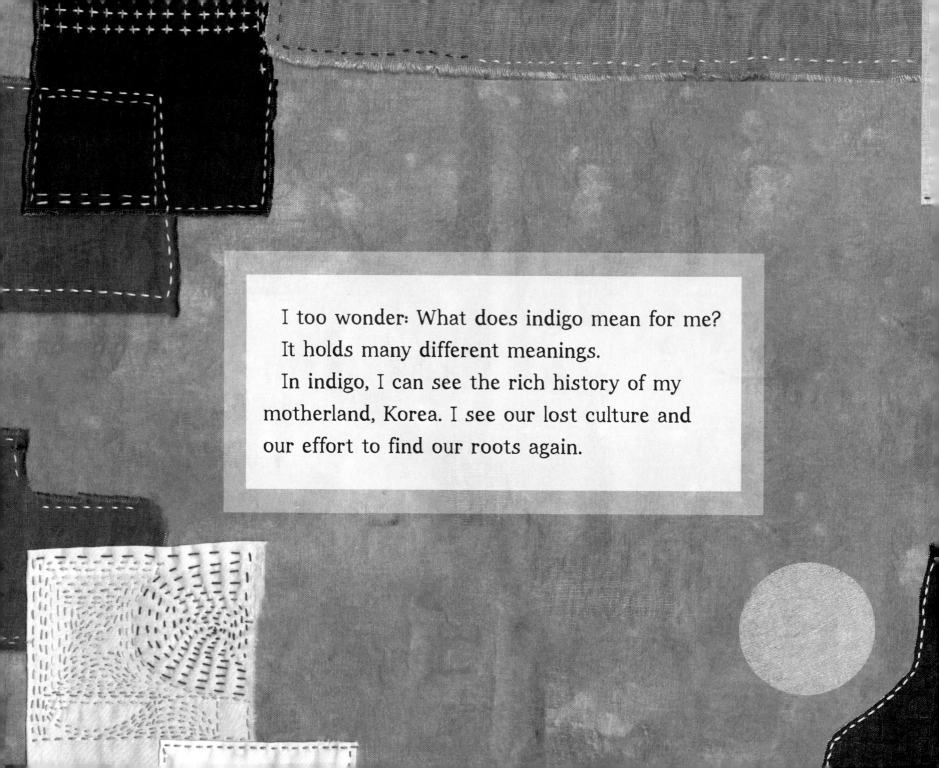

I too wonder: What **does** indigo mean for me?
It holds many **different** meanings.
In indigo, I can see the rich history of my
motherland, Korea. I see our lost culture and
our effort to find our roots again.

But in the United States and other countries, indigo also has a painful past.

For some people, indigo has been a symbol of blood, sweat, and tears—and exploitation.

People have often fought over indigo because it was worth so much money. Many people have been enslaved because of indigo, forced to leave their homes and land to work on indigo farms owned by others.

It is important to remember the pain along with the joy. Now, as my friends and I work in our garden together, we hope we can turn all those tears into love and care for others.

When fall comes, bright pink-and-white flowers bloom on the indigo plants. Bugs gorge themselves on the nectar of the flowers. "Don't drink too much, Mr. Bumblebee!"

Then in the late fall, we harvest indigo seeds
from the flowers and share them with our
friends and neighbors who helped us earlier
in the year.

We feel indigo love spreading as we share
our seeds, and I think of my friend who first
gave a handful of seeds to me.

When winter comes, it is silent in the garden, but we stay busy indoors creating indigo art and talking about our dreams for the world.

On those cozy winter days, I sometimes think back to
when I was a young girl. Little did I know then that the
color blue would open a whole new world of wonder to me!
I hope you, too, will find the magic seeds that open your
eyes and heart to the world.

More About Indigo

Indigo dye is extracted from not just one species of plant, but from a handful of species found in different parts of the world. Jjok, the species I have described in this story, is known by the scientific name *Polygonum tinctorium* and is sometimes called Japanese indigo.

Isatis

Isatis tinctoria, also called woad, is a species of flowering perennials that have been widely cultivated in Europe, Central Asia, and East Asia. Today, woad is widespread in portions of the Western United States, where it isconsidered a weed. Woad was once the most common source of indigo dyes in Europe, but has now been surpassed in popularity by a similar plant family called *Indigofera tinctoria*.

Polygonum tinctorium

The plant mentioned in this book. This is an annual plant with a long history in East Asia. Nowadays, it is also popular with gardeners and dyers in the US and elsewhere around the world.

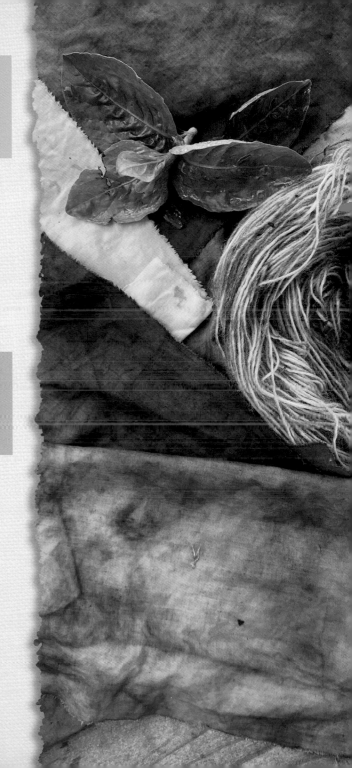

Strobilanthes cusia

This perennial plant is also known as Assam indigo. It thrives in the tropical regions of Asian countries such as India, Thailand, and Vietnam, as well as in China and Japan. In addition to its value for dyeing, Assam indigo is also used for treating sore throat, fever, and for other medicinal purposes.

Indigofera

The Indigofera genus is made up of many different plant species. Of these, *Indigofera tinctoria* and *Indigofera suffruticosa* are the ones most often cultivated for their blue pigments for dyeing. Another nickname for the plants of this genus is tropical indigo because they grow so well in the warmer climates of West Africa, South Asia, Mexico, and the southern United States.

Jjok and Korean History

In Korea, the culturally rich city of Naju is the center of traditional indigo dyeing. Naju is blessed with plenty of water, fertile soil, and a temperate climate, which makes a perfect environment to grow jjok (쪽). If you visit Naju today, you can see how Koreans have made indigo dye since ancient times.

The long history of traditional jjok dyeing in Korea goes back to sometime during the Three Kingdoms period (57 BC–AD 668). Since then, many sad events have occurred that have endangered the jjok tradition along with all other aspects of Korean culture. One of the biggest such events was the Korean War (1950–1953), which divided the country into two. The destruction of numerous farms across the entire Korean peninsula brought jjok farming to a complete halt. It seemed that one of Korea's ancient cultural traditions was about to be lost.

It took thirty years of hard work by the Korean government and individual farmers to revive the cultivation of jjok. In recent times, the Korean government has designated the most knowledgeable indigo dye masters, and the indigo dye process itself, as living national treasures that it hopes to protect, preserve, and pass down to the people of future generations.

You can still feel the love, joy, and pride of Koreans as the deep-blue-dyed clothes hang high all across the fields of Naju today.

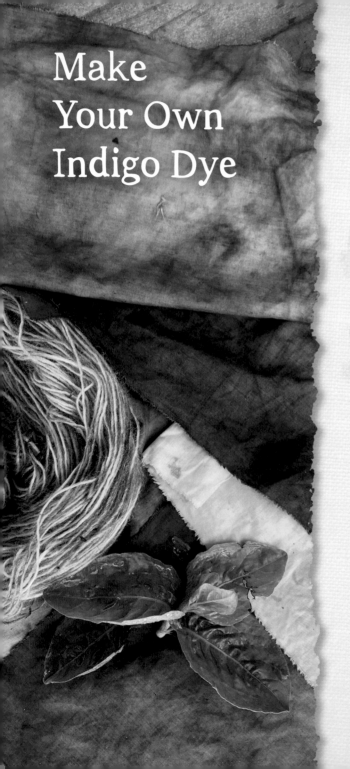

Make Your Own Indigo Dye

You can grow indigo plants at home and play with the leaves. Do you want to find the Real Blue in the leaves yourself? Here are two traditional methods from ancient East Asia.

Indigo Leaf Pounding Method

Supplies

- white 100% cotton cloth
- hard wooden board
- hammer
- fresh indigo leaves
- tape

1. Lay the cotton cloth flat on a wooden board.

2. Tape a leaf flat to the cloth, placing tape across both the leaf tip and stem.

3. Turn the cloth over, so that the leaf is now on the underside, keeping the cloth flat, and pound the leaf evenly with a hammer.

4. Remove the leaf from the cloth. You will now see the image of the leaf as a shadowlike stain on the cloth. The stain will be green at first, but with a little time—and exposure to the oxygen in the air—it will turn blue!

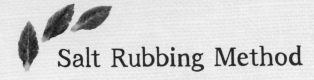

Salt Rubbing Method

Supplies

- a handful of fresh indigo leaves
- a stainless steel bowl
- sea salt
- a teaspoon
- a pair of disposable gloves
- a piece of natural fabric (cotton or silk)

1. Place freshly harvested indigo leaves in the stainless steel bowl.

2. Pour a teaspoon of sea salt into the bowl and, wearing gloves, massage the salt into the leaves.

3. After a couple of minutes, a turquoise liquid will begin to seep out of the leaves.

4. Put the cloth in the bowl and massage the cloth and leaves together.

5. The cloth will start to turn green and turquoise in color. Leave the cloth out for two hours to give it time to oxygenate and become the Real Blue. Then rinse the newly colorful cloth in cold water.

Making the Real Blue
FROM GREEN INDIGO LEAVES

There is more than one way to extract blue dye from indigo plants. In Japan, for example, harvested indigo leaves are dried and composted to create a substance called Sukumo, which looks just like wood chips and can be stored for long periods of time. In this book, I have described a very different method: the water extraction process traditionally used in Korea.

Tunisia

United States

Congo/
Central Africa

Nigeria

Mexico

Guatemala

Cameroon

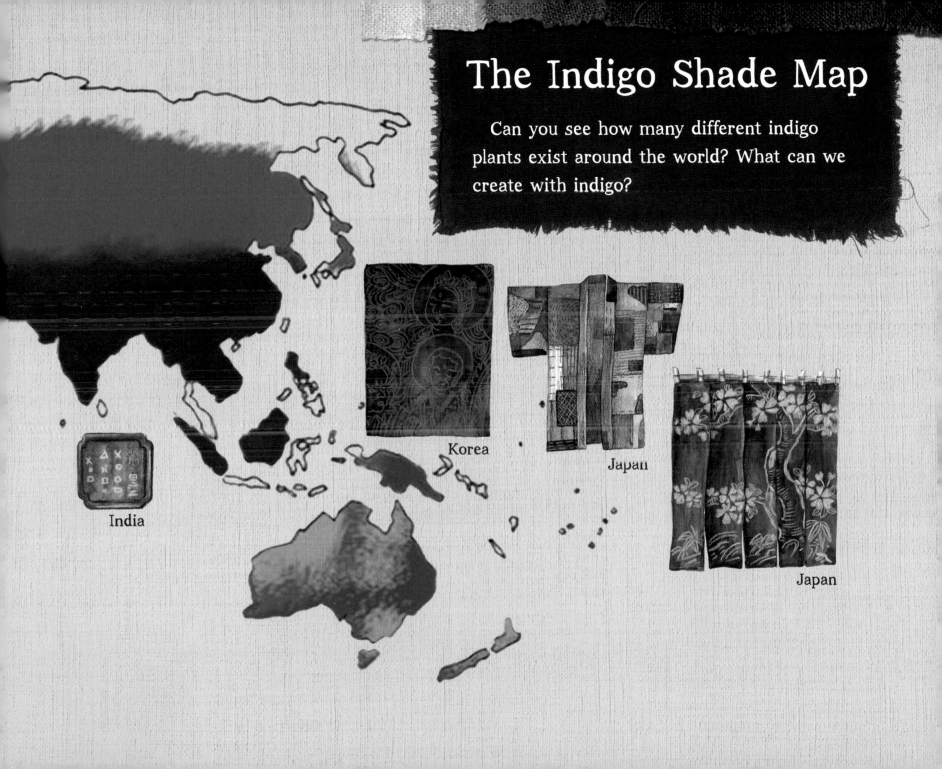

The Indigo Shade Map

Can you see how many different indigo plants exist around the world? What can we create with indigo?

India

Korea

Japan

Japan

For those who join my indigo and life journey.
Special thanks to you, Indigo Mom. —R.C.

Text and illustrations copyright © 2023 by Rosa Chang

mineditionUS
An imprint of Astra Books for Young Readers, a division of Astra Publishing House
astrapublishinghouse.com
Printed in Malaysia

ISBN: 978-1-6626-5065-9 (hc)
ISBN: 978-1-6626-5066-6 (eBook)

Library of Congress Control Number: 2022901206

First edition

10 9 8 7 6 5 4 3 2 1

Design by Honee Jang
The text is set in Rosa Chang's Indigo and Palmer Lake Print regular.
The titles are set in Rosa Chang's Indigo.
The illustrations were done in watercolor paint and hand-dyed indigo fabric and rendered digitally.